RAILWAYS
OF
HUNTINGDONSHIRE
(THE FIFTIES AND SIXTIES)

RAILWAYS OF HUNTINGDONSHIRE

(THE FIFTIES AND SIXTIES)

Eric Sawford

S.B. Publications

By the same author:
British Railways Steam in the Fifties (Alan Sutton)
British Railways Steam in the Sixties (Alan Sutton)
Steam Locomotives 1955; Eastern, North Eastern and Scottish (60000 - 69999) (Alan Sutton)

To my wife, Noreen, for many hours of word processing, checking seemingly endless facts, figures and often to her strange sounding railway terms.

First published in 1995 by S.B. Publications
c/o 19 Grove Road, Seaford, East Sussex BN25 1TP

ISBN 1 85770 076 7

Typeset and Printed by Island Press Ltd.
3 Cradle Hill Industrial Estate, Seaford, East Sussex, BN25 3JE
Tel: 01323 490222

CONTENTS

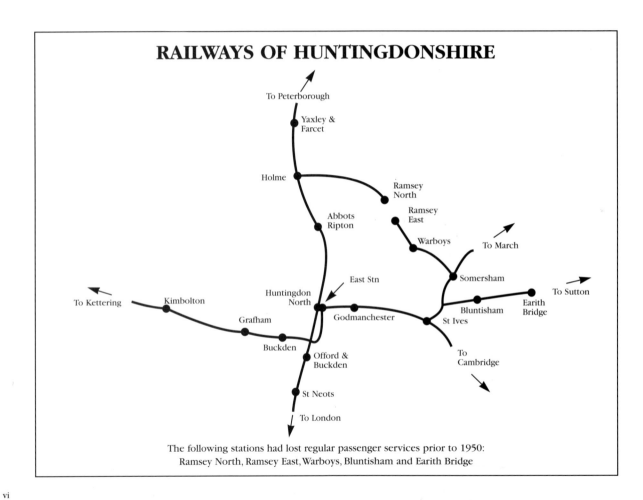

RAILWAYS OF HUNTINGDONSHIRE

To Peterborough

Yaxley & Farcet

Holme

Ramsey North

Ramsey East

Abbots Ripton

Warboys

To March

East Stn

Somersham

Huntingdon North

To Kettering

Kimbolton

Godmanchester

Earith Bridge

To Sutton

Grafham

Bluntisham

St Ives

Buckden

Offord & Buckden

To Cambridge

St Neots

To London

The following stations had lost regular passenger services prior to 1950:
Ramsey North, Ramsey East, Warboys, Bluntisham and Earith Bridge

INTRODUCTION

Over the last few years many more people have taken up residence in the area once known as the County of Huntingdonshire, resulting in considerable interest in the railways. This title covers the old county boundary and illustrates the scene as it was during the fifties and early sixties. While a number of the pictures may well surprise some people who were not familiar with the area at that time, for those who were – it will doubtless bring back many pleasant memories.

At the start of the fifties the county did not boast many railway stations that still had a regular passenger service, just thirteen in fact, of which two now remain! In addition there were a number still intact which on rare occasions were used for excursion trains and specials, the two Ramsey stations, the Great Northern branch from Holme to Ramsey North and the Great Eastern line from Somersham to Ramsey East via Warboys, also the Needingworth - Sutton line. All of these were normally used for goods traffic only at this time.

Most railway interest was centred on the East Coast Main Line which extended through the county for approximately twenty four miles. During the fifties the majority of express trains were handled by the famous Gresley *Pacifics* or V2 2-6-2s. The streamlined A4s were always the most popular, among these from King's Cross depot were the record breaking *Mallard*, *Wild Swan* and *Silver Link* often to be seen thundering through on principal expresses. With the re-introduction of the non stop King's Cross - Edinburgh service Haymarket depot A4s were to be seen. These included No. 60009 *Union of South Africa*, *Empire of India* and *Merlin* all taking an equal share with London based *Top Link* A4s.

The main line through the county did not present any problems for locomotives, south of Huntingdon it was undulating with a short section of 1 in 200, there was a speed restriction for the Offord curves. North of Huntingdon the line rose on a 1 in 200 gradient almost to Abbots Ripton, followed by a level section as it crossed the Fens.

One of the many lines to close nationwide during the late fifties was the cross country route from Kettering to Cambridge. This line entered the county at Kimbolton running through Grafham and Buckden to Huntingdon East station and on to Godmanchester and St Ives, where it joined the March - Cambridge line. Shortly after leaving St Ives the Huntingdonshire county boundary was crossed.

Just north of St Ives was Needingworth Junction, with a line running from here to Sutton, within the county were stations at Bluntisham and Earith Bridge both having lost their passenger service in the thirties. As with the two Ramsey branches, excursion traffic occasionally ran over the route and in most cases the stations were used. These trains were specials to Yarmouth Races, or to the coast in the summertime.

Only the main line still remains, very little is to be seen at any of the other locations mentioned indicating that a railway even existed. Long since gone are the interesting, often flower decked, wayside stations. The old county could only boast a single road locomotive shed at Huntingdon East, where this once stood is now the domain of heavy lorries and cars. Signal boxes, once a lineside feature, now consist of large power boxes, only a few, controlling busy level crossings remain, one example being at Offord.

Although primarily interested in locomotives, fortunately I did record on film many of the local everyday railway scenes, which when printed, seemed in many cases as just yesterday instead of forty years ago. I have not gone into a detailed history of the lines construction, or for that matter, listed details of the locomotives to be seen. Having put together a representative selection of my own photographs (with just one exception) leaving the pictures themselves to tell the story of all those years ago.

1. THE EAST COAST MAIN LINE

The line from just south of St Neots to near Peterborough presented few problems for locomotives. However, the speed restrictions for Offord curves were always carefully observed. The line from Huntingdon rose in a 1 in 200 gradient to almost Abbots Ripton. A few miles further on was one of the fast sections of track, being absolutely level for approximately five miles, this gave the opportunity for the locomotives on the principal expresses to show their paces before reaching the numerous brickworks with their accompanying yards and sidings to be seen at this time, just south of Peterborough.

Within the County of Huntingdonshire on the main line in the early fifties were six stations. Those at Offord and Buckden, Abbots Ripton, Holme, Yaxley and Farcet, long since gone. Leaving just two, Huntingdon and St Neots.

Looking at this picture could easily give the impression it was taken in LNER days. The date was in fact the 27 September 1953. The two famous 'Ivatt Atlantics' were working the southbound Plant Centenarian, the leading engine is a C2 class 4-4-2 No. 990 Henry Oakley, behind is C1 No. 251, both are part of the National Collection at York Museum. Doncaster works where both were built, was known as 'The Plant'. The return train was headed by No. 60014 Silver Link. This interesting picture was taken near Abbots Ripton.

Offord and Buckden station was still in regular use when this picture was taken on the 30th January 1955. The station closed on the 2 February 1959. Note the signal box controlling the gates, also the long footbridge with access to the platforms. Apart from the crossing with lifting barriers and small signal box now on the right hand side, nothing remains.

The Thompson L1 class 2-6-4Ts were commonplace on the King's Cross to Peterborough local services during the early fifties. No. 67746 running bunker first leaves Huntingdon with an afternoon service on the 16 March 1954. The building on the left-hand side was the Timekeeper's office. The L1s were later replaced on these services by B1 class 4-6-0s.

V2 class 2-6-2s were frequently used on express trains, not only to replace a failed or unavailable locomotive, but on many occasions they were rostered to work the train in the normal way. In this picture No. 60966 thunders through Huntingdon on the 17 September 1954 at the head of a Newcastle to London express. In the yards an L1 2-6-4T awaits time to work south with a pick-up goods.

This picture shows the River Ouse bridge south of Huntingdon; in the distance can just be seen the temporary signal box put in for engineering work. Note the concrete platelayers hut on the left, once a familiar sight on the main line.

The class 55 diesel locomotives known as 'Deltics' made their appearance in 1961. Within a short time they were working express trains alongside the earlier class 40s. The remaining steam locomotives were still to be seen in the early sixties on express trains, but the writing was on the wall, within a short time the steadily increasing numbers of diesels took over completely. Here Meld heads north through St Neots in March 1966. The station can be seen in the background.

Just south of Huntingdon station were these two sets of signals. The two posts with double arms controlling down main and slow, crossovers from main to slow and vice versa were controlled by the single arms. The two posts without arms were originally used to give connections to Huntingdon East Station. The A4 was heading north with a relief express. (1 August 1954).

A4 No. 60033 Seagull *seen here on the 1 August 1954 was in charge of the 9.39am to King's Cross. Huntingdon did not have anything like the frequency of trains to London that it has today. The 9.39am was a fast train, regular commuters to the Capital were almost unknown forty years ago.*

The legendary No. 60103 Flying Scotsman *was a regular sight at Huntingdon. Here the A3 heads south with an express on 4 August 1954. This engine was later to receive a double chimney and German-type smoke deflectors. Note the white painted board in the foreground, this was the marker for the despatcher on the travelling Post Office trains to swing out his pouches for Huntingdon. The first TPO set can just be seen in the distance.*

Between 1934-6 Nigel Gresley built six P2 class 2-8-2 locomotives principally for use between Edinburgh and Aberdeen. In 1943 the first of the class was rebuilt as a 'Pacific' with the other five in the following year, all were then allocated in England and classified A2/2 class. Three were based at York and three at New England. Here one of the later engines, No. 60506 Wolf of Badenoch leaves Huntingdon with a King's Cross express on the 10 January 1954. The three New England locomotives were a regular sight at Huntingdon, the York engines also appearing from time to time.

B1 No. 61203 was a King's Cross engine when seen heading south with a fast goods on 1 August 1954. Locomotives of this class were frequently employed on semi-fast passenger, parcels and fast goods traffic. During the fifties a King's Cross B1 would be the usual motive power for the Sunday Skegness excursions. Note the two crossovers in the foreground, nearest the camera is the Huntingdon yards to 'up slow', behind is the 'up main' to slow line. Many goods trains being turned slow road after passing through Huntingdon station.

B1 No. 61097 had plenty of steam to spare as it ran down the 1 in 200 bank towards Huntingdon. The B1 was heading a Peterborough to King's Cross local on the 28 April 1954. Although it would appear to be four tracks, the line on the far side was in fact a siding at this time.

New England depot had a sizable number of the WD 2-8-0 locomotives in its allocation in the early fifties. Their duties including heavy coal traffic to Ferme Park London and normal freight trains. With the arrival of the Standard Class 9F 2-10-0s a number of WDs were transferred away. Those that remained were still to be seen south of Peterborough until steam finished on this section. No. 90439 is seen here heading north at Huntingdon on the 4 August 1954.

K3 No. 61824 restarts a southbound fast goods from Huntingdon on 11 July 1954 after taking water. The engine was allocated to Colwick depot (Nottingham). The 2-6-0 K3 class were designed by Nigel Gresley and were classified mixed traffic locomotives, equally at home on goods or passenger turns. These engines were easily recognised by their large boilers. When due for works overhaul they had the reputation of being rough riding.

Only on very rare occasions would the opportunity arise of photographing something a little different, this was the case on the 29 July 1952.
A2/3 No. 60500 Edward Thompson *had just arrived with a King's Cross to Peterborough train when V2 No. 60800* Green Arrow *rolled in on the*
slow line heading a pick-up goods. For just a few moments they stood side by side. The V2 is the sole example of this famous Nigel Gresley design
to survive into preservation.

At the south end of Huntingdon station was the large water tank, which judging from the position of the contents indicator (if working) was either not in use or pretty low. I can never remember this chimney showing signs of use. This picture taken on 25 December 1955 shows the Huntingdon Pilot J15 No. 65451 in the siding. Presumably the small locomotive depot was temporarily out of use; as it was unusual for the engine to stand at this location.

Ex. LMS design locomotives were very unusual on the East Coast Main Line during the fifties, not so a few years later, when towards the end of steam Black 5s, 8Fs and 'Jubilees' were seen on freight workings. On this occasion, 15 August 1955 No. 42328 was working a pick-up goods. Two of these Fowler 2-6-4Ts were allocated to Hitchin depot at the time.

One of New England depots V2 2-6-2s No. 60832 arrives at Huntingdon on the 11 February 1955, working a heavy coal train to Ferme Park. On occasions 'Pacifics' would turn up on coal trains, even the streamlined A4s were certainly not unknown on such duties. Usual motive power at this time was the WD 2-8-0s and Standard 9F 2-10-0s.

The front of Huntingdon station has generally changed little since this picture was taken on 30 January 1955. The many notice boards to be seen at that time advertising day returns to London and in the summer months excursions to Skegness which were very popular in the fifties. The station nameboard at this time read Huntingdon North.

Huntingdon North station September 1956, the buildings and platform on the right, together with the footbridge, have long since been replaced. The up side, although considerably modified is still in use. At this time the three main platforms existed, this is now two with a bay on the London side.

Framed by the road bridge at Huntingdon North A1 class 'Pacific' No. 60136 Alcazar *heads a lightweight Sunday King's Cross to Peterborough stopping train on 3 August 1952. In the background is one of the articulated suburban coach sets. The A1 was completed at Darlington works in November 1948 and withdrawn in May 1963.*

This picture has been included as it shows several once commonplace items of railway equipment. The wooden structure near the locomotive is a loading gauge used to check clearances on unusual loads. In the distance near the water tank is a hand operated crane, seldom used in the fifties. The locomotive on this occasion was L1 class 2-6-4T No. 67744 of Hitchin depot. 17 September 1954.

The World Speed Record Holder for a steam locomotive No. 60022 Mallard *was usually seen at the head of express trains as they thundered through Huntingdon. It was however by no means uncommon for the 'top link' King's Cross engines to work duties such as this three coach Sunday local passenger train on 4 July 1954. Fortunately this splendid locomotive is among the A4s preserved. It is part of the National Collection on display at York Railway Museum.*

Huntingdon North, 9 May 1954, photographed from the end of the East Station platform. The large goods shed is on the left, some of the many wagons present at that time can be seen in the yards. The rather unusual signal was very important as it indicated main line or turning slow road. This message was also conveyed to drivers at the far end of the station. Note also the signal wires and point rodding on the right hand side of the picture, once a very important part of the railway scene.

This picture will be familiar to many present day passengers as the area is now part of the car park. The roadway was the approach to the East Station which was located behind the photographer. Several coal merchants had the sidings in the 'up' yard. The buffer stops of several lines can just be seen in this picture taken on 28 August 1954.

A4 class 'Pacifics' were mostly in superb condition in the early fifties. The long backlog of locomotive maintenance through the war years had been eliminated. The track had been restored to pre-war condition enabling timings to be improved. No. 60006 Sir Ralph Wedgewood *was just leaving Huntingdon on 9 May 1954. Nineteen A4s including No. 60006 were allocated to King's Cross depot which was widely known as 'Top Shed'.*

A4 No. 60026 Miles Beevor *speeds through Abbots Ripton with a northbound express. The up and down platforms were staggered and joined by a footbridge. After the station itself had been demolished Abbots Ripton signal box stood in stark isolation for many years. Driving along the road seen at the right hand side, today reveals a very different picture of this spot.*

Most Engineers trains were worked by J6 class locomotives. No. 64224 was a New England engine, one of the large number allocated there. Note the veteran six wheeled composite coach, many such interesting vehicles were used on Engineers, signal and telegraph trains. At the time most enthusiasts paid little attention to them. No. 64224 was photographed on 9 May 1954 alongside the long loading bay which existed on the northern side of the railway bridge.

V2 No. 60906 heading a mixed goods was just about to rejoin the main line at Abbots Ripton heading for London on the 3 October 1953. This station was closed on the 15 September 1958 and later completely demolished, the site now gives no indication that a station had ever existed. Note the oil lamps on the platform.

This view shows the East Coast Main Line in August 1952, on the northern side of the road bridge. Note the small oil depot which existed on the left hand side of the picture and the cattle loading bay immediately in front of Huntingdon No. 2 box. The line in the centre was a short siding under the road bridge. The signal has two repeaters halfway along its length indicating either main line or turning to slow road immediately through the station.

This class of diesel was commonly known as 'Baby Deltics', they were a daily sight at Huntingdon in the early sixties, working local passenger trains. No. D5908 is about to cross over to the 'up line' ready for its return working to King's Cross. This class was not large, and does not have an example in preservation. September 1961.

Huntingdon station looking north 8 April 1956. The scene is very different today, the road bridge still remains, overshadowed by the modern concrete structure carrying the heavily used A14. Long gone are the imposing array of semaphore signals. Note also the water crane which was located at the end of the platform and frequently used in steam days. The station lighting at the time was gas. Huntingdon No. 2 signal box can just be seen through the arch on the right-hand side.

Tank locomotives working in the London area were normally run under their own steam to and from Doncaster Works. Many of these movements took place at night or during quiet periods. Sunday mornings would often see locomotives proceeding north, invariably they would have to take water at Huntingdon. J52 class No. 68819 had just done so and was continuing its journey when photographed on 7 February 1955. The locomotive was withdrawn in June 1956 after fifty-seven years service.

This picture taken in the cutting to the north of Huntingdon on 20 September 1959 shows widening work in progress to add the 'up slow', after only a few years it was removed. Although four tracks exist at Huntingdon, up trains are now turned to the slow line about half a mile north of the station.

2. HUNTINGDON EAST AND THE KETTERING – CAMBRIDGE LINE

Although this line had only three passenger trains each way daily, and very little goods traffic in the fifties, it was of considerable interest to the enthusiast.

Motive Power in the early fifties was a few elderly 2F Midland 0-6-0s, with examples of the lightweight Ivatt 2-6-0s and later two of the very similar Standard Class 2MT 2-6-0s. One train was worked throughout by a Cambridge depot J15, otherwise the only other class I can recall was an Ivatt 2MT 2-6-2T working an inspection saloon.

Within the county boundary were six stations on this cross country route. Kimbolton, Grafham. Buckden, Huntingdon East, Godmanchester and St Ives.

Huntingdon East station from the steps of No. 1 signal box, 17 October 1954, the Midland line is to the right. The other two platforms to the left, of which only one received occasional use by a RAF leave train. Up until the early fifties a two coach service was provided from Huntingdon to St Ives worked by the 'Pilot'. Note also the wide platform with its gravel surface. Where this station once stood is part of the car park for the present Huntingdon Station.

During the summer months a heavy train ran from the Cambridgeshire fruit-growing districts to Kettering, and onward to various markets. Due to weight restrictions on the River Ouse bridge, locomotive double heading was prohibited. The train ran to Huntingdon No. 1 box where a pilot engine was waiting to commence the journey over the undulating line to Kettering. No. 46401 had just crossed the river on a sunny evening, 10 August 1954. This train did not present too many problems for a 2MT single handed, but with the Midland 2F 06-0s it was a very different matter – on many occasions I have watched one struggling to reach Huntingdon East, and on more than one instance the fireman walking in front to place grit and sand on the track to give the locomotive a grip, which was invariably sending a plume of smoke high in the air.

Huntingdon East had connections to the main line. For a period a Royal Air Force leave train was operated from the station to King's Cross on a Friday evening. L1 No. 67745 was on the duty on 2 August 1954. The train reporting number (571) chalked on the smokebox door. The stock was made up of one of the articulated suburban sets. Although this locomotive was fitted with electric lighting, oil lamps can be seen in use.

The wooden trestle bridge over the River Ouse looking towards Godmanchester station 8 March 1954. Due to the condition of the bridge the track between Godmanchester and Huntingdon had been singled. A speed restriction of 10m.p.h. was in force. Weight restrictions having applied for a great many years. In the background is Childs and Hall boatyard and the once familiar tall mill building. Despite the age of the bridge, the large timbers sunk into the river bed did not yield easily to the demolition contractor's equipment..

The last steam locomotive to work at Godmanchester was J15 No. 65420 on track lifting duties. The line had already gone almost to the station when this picture was taken on the 30 August 1961. As no facilities remained at Huntingdon the locomotive ran back to New England depot nightly. This J15 was one of the class fitted with steam brake only.

Godmanchester level crossing, although the road was open no traffic appears in the picture; how different now. On the left is the road entrance to the station sidings and goods shed. The small hut was Messrs Coote and Warren's Coal Office; note the coal yard on the right. The crossing keeper's hut can also be seen behind the buffer stop. The line itself had been reduced to single track when this picture was taken on 8 March 1954.

The J15 class locomotives which were supplied to Huntingdon on the regular rota were usually from Nos. 65442/51/57/61/74/5/7. Only on rare occasions would a different member of the class appear. One of these instances was on 10 April 1953 when No. 65405 was on the duty, this engine was fitted with a tender cab and was more usually found on the Colne Valley line. Note the large white Great Eastern section disc in use in place of the handlamp. No. 65405 had just crossed the River Ouse, notice the smoke coming from the Hosiery Mill chimney, now private residential property and 10m.p.h. speed restriction on the bridge.

The approach to Godmanchester photographed from the St Ives end, 16 July 1954. The station and signal box can be seen in the distance. The large mill building has long since disappeared. The site is now occupied by industrial and local authority buildings. On the far left of the picture wagons standing in the goods yard can be seen. Godmanchester was still handling a considerable amount of goods traffic at this time.

Huntingdon East with Ivatt 2-6-0 No. 46401 departing with the 3.09pm service to Cambridge. Only three trains travelled in each direction on weekdays. On Saturday the same number ran with the exception that the last departure from Kettering was not until 8.12pm, arriving Huntingdon East at 9.05pm and Cambridge 9.50pm. No regular Sunday services were operated, although on a few occasions the line was opened especially for excursions and special trains.

With a friendly wave from Driver Golden of Kettering depot, 2MT No. 46496 leaves Godmanchester on 16 July 1954 with the return goods working. The crossing gates were already open. As will be seen from this picture the platforms at Godmanchester were not directly facing. The signal box roof can just be seen on the right of the picture above the locomotive's cab. Note the carefully tended and colourful flower beds on the left.

Ivatt 2MT No. 46496 had only the guards van for its return working to Kettering on the 16 July 1954. This was often the case, although wagons would usually be collected along the route home. The fireman climbs aboard the locomotive as it completes shunting at Godmanchester. In those days several sidings were still in use at the station, including connections to the mill.

Huntingdon East Station, September 1961. The buildings on the island platform and footbridge have completely disappeared. The Midland line was in situ and complete with signals. On the far side the water crane was still there and would have been used occasionally by the locomotive lifting the line from St Ives. On the platform a pair of redundant crossing gates await despatch. In the far right-hand side of the picture Huntingdon Grammar School buildings can be seen, these were destroyed by fire and demolished a short time ago.

A Christmas Day picture, at Huntingdon East looking towards the main line. Note the gas lighting and fancy ironwork on the roof supporting pillars. Where this station once stood is now part of the present station car parking facilities. The end of the right-hand platform was a favourite spot for railway enthusiasts in those days, not just locals, but it was also a familiar location to enthusiasts from Cambridge and elsewhere.

Christmas Day 1955 dawned bright and clear after overnight rain. The conditions resulting in this interesting picture taken at Huntingdon East looking towards Godmanchester. Many items of note appear, including check rails due to the very tight curves, the water crane used daily, a regular sight at most stations in steam days. The interesting footbridge and signals of various types, with in the distance the small locomotive shed.

The small turntable at the back of Huntingdon shed was a tight fit for a 2MT 2-6-0 and extremely hard work for the engine crew. No. 46496 was photographed on the 17 June 1952. The locomotive working the Midland goods and also the pilot engine for the fruit train in summer used the turntable. Only on very rare occasions was it used by the J15 allocated on a rota basis from Cambridge.

Prior to the arrival of the Ivatt 2MT 2-6-0s the passenger and goods trains on the Kettering-Cambridge line were worked by these elderly Johnson designed Midland Railway 2F 0-6-0s. The Ivatt 2MT took over most of the passenger services on their arrival at Kettering depot in 1946. Until sufficient numbers became available the 2F 0-6-0s regularly appeared on the goods. No. 58193 takes water at Huntingdon East on the 17 June 1952. Locomotives of this class were still receiving attention at Derby works at this time, as was likely in this case, judging by the repainted smokebox and chimney.

Nearly at journey's end with a sizable load, J15 No. 65477 heads the pick up goods near to Huntingdon East on 25 May 1954. After leaving the East Station the train would be set back across the main line into the goods yards. No. 65477 was built at the Stratford Works of the Great Eastern Railway, being completed in August 1913 and was withdrawn from service in February 1960.

The first departure from Cambridge daily for Kettering was worked by an engine from that depot. For several years No. 65390 was the regular locomotive. Although on occasions other members of the class would be used, if the usual engine was unavailable. The J15 worked back with the last train of the day. No. 65475 was on the duty on the 28 April 1954 and is seen here departing from Huntingdon East, the low evening sun highlighting the inside of the rather spartan cab.

The 7 March 1953 was a quiet day for the St Ives - Huntingdon local goods. J15 No. 65438 having a good head of steam stands ready for departure from Godmanchester. The locomotive was fitted with a tender cab and only occasionally sent to Huntingdon, its more normal duties being on the Colne Valley line. No. 65438 was built at Stratford Works in 1899 and withdrawn from service in June 1958.

Ivatt 2MT No. 46403 approaches Godmanchester on the 13 July 1954 on its way back to Kettering. The train was just crossing one of the river backwaters, crossed like most on the Huntingdon to St Ives section by a wooden trestle bridge. These bridges resulted in weight restrictions on the line. It was the main river bridge at Huntingdon that presented the major problems in the last years.

Godmanchester signal box, J15 No. 65467 had just arrived on its way to St Ives on 8 March 1954. Traffic was often light in this direction, on the return twenty to twenty-five wagons were a frequent load. The trip to St Ives usually took two to two and a half hours, running Monday to Fridays. No. 65457 was one of the regular locomotives at Huntingdon, remaining in service until February 1962.

Hitchin J6 0-6-0 No. 64240 was short of water on the 18 August 1954, taking the rather unusual step of setting back into the East Station platform. The J6 class was a Gresley design introduced in 1911 by the Great Northern Railway, with over one hundred of these very useful locomotives being built. During the fifties J6s were almost a daily sight at Huntingdon, mostly on engineers' trains.

Huntingdon East 28 August 1954. The two connections onto the main line can be clearly seen. On the far left is the double aspect Midland line signal and the line running down to cross under the East Coast Main Line. Note No. 1 box with its large telegraph poles at either end, these poles were a feature of the railway lineside during this period. Where most of these items once stood is now part of the station car park.

The locomotive which was to pilot the fruit train from Huntingdon to Kettering usually came up double heading the 3.09pm arrival from Kettering. After turning at the small shed it usually had two or three hours to wait for the arrival of its train which was normally between 7pm and 7.30pm. The pilot engine on the 28 August 1954 was Standard Class 2MT No. 78020. Note the 'fixed distant' warning of the two crossings ahead.

2MT class No. 46495 arrives at St Ives on the 24 June 1954 and was about to take the Kettering line as indicated by the signal. The train having a full brake coach in its make up was unusual, as normally it would consist of three or four coaches only. Kettering depot eventually had a total of ten of these lightweight 2-6-0s, eight Ivatt and two of the later Standard design.

The afternoon train from Kettering pictured at St Ives, ready to complete the final section to Cambridge on the 14 August 1954. The locomotive in charge was Standard Class 2MT No. 78020, one of two of this design allocated to Kettering depot during this period. Note the St Ives Junction signal box at the end of the platform and the two young train spotters.

After the line from Kettering crossed under the East Coast Main line it ran parallel for approximately one mile, initially at a lower level, then climbing up to Huntingdon East. This picture shows the bridge that enabled the line to cross the River Ouse. Note the reflection in the fairly still water when this picture was taken on the 29 April 1954.

This picture of the Midland line platform at Huntingdon East station gives an idea of the sharp curve. As can be clearly seen the track was fitted with a continuous check rail, a severe speed restriction of 10m.p.h. was also imposed with a warning board to the left of the picture. The Kettering - Cambridge service was to remain for another five years after this 1954 photograph was taken.

Huntingdon No. 1 signal box was responsible for the main line and also Huntingdon East. Here we see the signalman and locomotive fireman exchanging the tablet as 2MT No. 46496 arrives from Kettering on 8 March 1955. Note the unusual two-way signal, also the platform built to enable the tablet to be exchanged easily.

The 'Midland Goods' ran from Kettering to Godmanchester, it was never very heavily loaded in the fifties. Midland 2F class 0-6-0 No. 58214 is seen passing Huntingdon shed with a lightweight train on its return journey, 19 July 1952. The 2Fs were soon completely replaced by the Ivatt 2-6-0s. No. 58214 had probably received a light works repair, judging by the repainted smokebox and chimney, this was often done on such occasions.

The line from Kettering ran under the main line a mile south of Huntingdon, crossed the River Ouse on its own bridge and then climbed up to Huntingdon East. This picture taken on 2 April 1956 shows 2MT No. 46444 nearing the Huntingdon No. 1 signal box where the single line tablet would be exchanged. Kettering shed received the first new Ivatt 2-6-0s to replace ageing Johnson Midland Railway locomotives. The more comfortable cab being particularly welcome in the new engines.

Buckden, 29 July 1952 with No. 46403 heading a Kettering - Cambridge train. This station was closed on 15 June 1959. The building was used as a private residence for many years, the signalbox was later removed for preservation. The other two stations in Huntingdonshire on this section, Grafham and Kimbolton, also closed on the same day.

Probably the last appearance of an E4 class 2-4-0 was on the 22 April 1957 when No. 62788 appeared on a weed-killing train. Very few E4s were still in service. No. 62788 had definitely seen better days. This locomotive was one of the small batch fitted with side window cabs for working over the exposed line to Penrith. E4s were a regular sight at Huntingdon in the late forties and very early fifties, during the fifties it was the J15 class which were the regular locomotives.

3. ST IVES AND THE HUNTINGDONSHIRE BRANCHES

St Ives was on the March - Cambridge line, known as the 'St Ives Loop'. Passenger services were in operation, although the line principally carried heavy goods traffic, thus avoiding Ely on the direct line.

Three branches were still operational in the early fifties all having lost their passenger services. Ramsey was served from Holme to Ramsey North. Another line running from Somersham to Ramsey East via. Warboys.

At Needingworth Junction a line ran to Sutton via. Bluntisham and Earith Bridge. Intermediate stations were still intact at the points mentioned and very occasionally used by excursion trains.

The J20 class 0-6-0s were designed by A J Hill for the Great Eastern Railway and introduced in 1930. Twenty five were built, all being taken over by British Railways at Nationalisation. Several members of the class were allocated to March depot including No. 64690, seen here passing St Ives on 18 August 1954. Note the low wagon next to the engine. This particular locomotive remained in service until September 1962.

'Sandringham Class' B17 No. 61619 Welbeck Abbey *heading the afternoon parcels to March stands at St Ives on 8 September 1954. While porters busily add onward parcel traffic, the driver takes the opportunity to have his picture taken with the locomotive. In the background can be seen the rather faded station nameboard reading St Ives change for Godmanchester and Huntingdon. Several types of locomotive were used on this train ranging from 'Sandringhams', 'Clauds' and on occasions K3 2-6-0s during the fifties.*

St Ives looking towards Cambridge on the 17 March 1954. The two lines on the far right of the picture lead onto the Huntingdon branch. In the distance on the left can be seen the diverging slow line towards Cambridge which was not used much during the fifties. Over on the far left behind the tall building was the Meadow Lane yard of Messrs W & J Glossop where at least one Sentinel steam wagon existed at this time. St Ives was on the March-Cambridge route known as the 'St Ives loop' used mainly by heavy freight traffic avoiding Ely.

K1 class 2-6-0 No. 62040 pictured carrying out shunting duties at St Ives on 28 August 1954. Several members of the K1 class were allocated to March during the fifties. Note also the considerable number of wagons to be seen in the goods yard. Seventy of the K1 class were built, being introduced in 1949, fortunately one example has survived into preservation, No. 62005 (now 2005) is to be found on the North Yorkshire Moors Railway.

Two 'Claud Hamilton' class 4-4-0s Nos. 62614/18 were retained for working Royal Trains. In 1946 No. 8783, soon to be renumbered 2614 and then 62614 on nationalisation, was repainted in LNER green livery, the other D16 receiving similar attention three years later. Both locomotives were a familiar sight at St Ives on local passenger workings. Here No. 62614 arrives with the afternoon train to March on 24 June 1954. Note the burnished ring on the smokebox door which was a feature of both locomotives. This engine was withdrawn in August 1958 and No. 62618 in November 1959. Unfortunately no example of the class with its long association with East Anglia has survived into preservation.

The J17 class 0-6-0s were frequent visitors to St Ives in the fifties. No. 65501, a Kings Lynn engine, was just about to continue its journey on the 24 June 1954. This particular locomotive was built as a J16 class in 1900 and later rebuilt to J17, it was fitted with steam brake only and was one of those running with a smaller tender. This engine remained in service until January 1958. One example of the J17 class has been preserved as part of the National Collection.

Meadow Lane crossing St Ives, K3 No. 61943 of March depot heads a mixed goods towards Cambridge on the 17 March 1954. The line can be seen curving away to the right. Many goods trains were routed via St Ives to avoid congestion on the direct line. Examples of the K3 class remained until the end of steam working at March depot, although some of the last survivors were stored out of use in the depot yard for a considerable time. No. 61943 was withdrawn with several others in September 1962.

Heading a lightweight goods through St Ives K3 No. 61886 heads for March. K3 class locomotives were mostly used on freight work but were occasionally to be seen on passenger trains. Although an example of this famous Nigel Gresley design would have been an ideal subject for preservation, none have in fact survived. No. 61886 was one of several examples of this very useful class of mixed traffic locomotives which were allocated to March depot. This particular engine was withdrawn in September 1962.

The afternoon Cambridge train headed by D16/3 No. 62569 awaits departure time at St Ives on the 1 July 1954. Note the locomotive is carrying one of the Great Eastern white discs instead of lamps still commonplace at this time. Most of the passenger services were worked by the D16 class, commonly known as 'Clauds'. This particular locomotive was nearing the end of its days, being withdrawn in November 1956, completing just over forty-eight years service.

Regular passenger services over the Needingworth Junction to Sutton line finished on 2 February 1931. When this picture was taken at Bluntisham on 16 September 1953, J15 No. 65474 was heading a five coach Yarmouth Races Excursion, one of the few specials to use this route during the fifties. The line was closed completely from Bluntisham to Sutton on the 6 October 1958 and from Needingworth Junction to Bluntisham on 5 October 1964. During the Second World War the route saw increased usage when various trains were diverted over the line. (Author's collection).

Regular passenger services on the Somersham to Ramsey East line were withdrawn on the 22 September 1930. This picture shows Ramsey East as it was on the 24 July 1955, the station building still surviving and with an old wagon body adjacent. In the fifties very occasional special passenger trains were worked over the branch, mainly to Yarmouth Races. Enthusiasts' specials were also run in the final years. Complete closure of the Warboys to Ramsey section was on 20 August 1957.

J17 No. 65562 was in charge of the Railway Correspondence and Travel Society 'Fensman' Rail Tour, photographed at Ramsey East on 24 July 1955. This particular J17 was a March engine and was used on several specials during its last years in service. Note the cleanliness of the locomotive and impressive headboard carried. The yard contained quite a number of vans at this time, in just over two years everything was finished.

The RCTS 'Fensman' on its way to Ramsey, pictured in typical Fenland scenery. The engine No. 65562 carried a small RCTS board on the tender and Great Eastern type white discs with express passenger headcode. Most of the train was made up of Gresley stock, each coach complete with nameboard. The locomotive was worked tender first on the inward journey as no turning facilities existed at Ramsey East.

This view of Ramsey North was taken on 24 July 1955 and shows the station buildings. Note the two levels of platform, several wagons are to be seen in various sidings. Sparse goods traffic was still worked to Ramsey North for another eighteen years, in the final years with diesel locomotives.

Ramsey North Station on the 24 July 1955. The Holme to Ramsey line was only open for goods traffic at this time, passenger services having ceased on the 6 October 1947. During its final years 'Railway Enthusiasts Specials' travelled over the branch, which was closed completely on the 2 July 1973.

4. MISCELLANEOUS

This section contains pictures of accidents and Travelling Post Office Lineside Equipment, together with photographs of some of the regular J15 class 0-6-0s from Cambridge depot. These locomotives were outstationed at Huntingdon for shunting and local goods working, using the small one road shed at Huntingdon East.

The New England depot 45 ton breakdown crane seen here in action lifting the J15s tender. At major depots a crane was often kept in light steam, the operator raising working pressure during the journey to the incident so as to arrive ready for immediate action. Motive power was provided by any available locomotive which was ready for the road, coaled and watered. Fitters from the depot manning the breakdown crane under the supervision of the locomotive Superintendent or deputy. When called to lift a heavy locomotive two cranes working together would be required.

While working the goods to St Ives on the 3 August 1955 J15 0-6-0 No. 65475 became derailed near Huntingdon locomotive shed, taking with it the first wagon. Assistance was summoned from New England depot, the breakdown train arriving behind WD 2-8-0 No. 90519. The WD propelled the crane into position through Huntingdon East station accompanied by much squealing of wheel flanges, due to the tight curve and check rails. In this picture the breakdown train crew assess the situation, a junior fireman having been given the job of watching the gauges on the locomotive which had a full head of steam.

This was the scene at Offord on the 8 October 1962 following the accident caused by A1 class 'Pacific' No. 60123 H A Ivatt heading the 8.50pm Kings Cross to Leeds goods, running into the back of the preceding 8.25pm Kings Cross - Newcastle while approaching Offord. As a result the main line was completely blocked. Breakdown cranes from Peterborough and Doncaster were required to lift the locomotive which was lying on its side, and removing the considerable number of smashed wagons, some of which had been totally destroyed. The breakdown set from Peterborough is seen here lifting another wagon clear of the debris.

By Sunday 9 October 1962 the locomotive and tender had been recovered and moved to a siding north of Offord crossing. The very considerable front end damage resulted in the engine being withdrawn and cut up at Doncaster Works. Unfortunately, no example of the forty nine strong A1 class has survived into preservation. Although 1994 was to see the commencement of a project to build a brand new locomotive of this design. The engine in this picture H A Ivatt was named after the famous Great Northern Railway Chief Mechanical Engineer from 1896-1911. Among his famous designs were the well known 4-4-2 'Atlantics'

This fine set of Great Northern somersault signals were among the last in use in the county. This picture taken on the 20 June 1953 announces a clear road for an express on the 'up main'. At this time signal boxes were a regular feature every few miles, note the long since demolished Paxton box in the background.

One of the regular Huntingdon pilots was No. 65451 seen in Huntingdon yards on the 31 August 1954. Note the Westinghouse Pump just forward of the cab, often these showed the damage caused by coal hammers, when used to free a sticking pump. The J15s, despite their size, were powerful engines and even up to their last days examples could still be seen on branch line passenger work. This particular locomotive was withdrawn in September 1959.

Huntingdon locomotive depot on the 23 October 1954. The J15 No. 65457 still carrying a Bay 1 board on the smokebox, probably left at Cambridge depot before it was sent over on a normal exchange. The locomotive coal supply was usually a single wagon, on some occasions it was loaded on the platform near the shed, at other times coal was shovelled straight into the locomotive tender, as was the case here judging by the small pile spilt between wagon and tender.

Huntingdon shed was in need of a tidy up on the 23 October 1954. The ashpit required cleaning out, and clinker lies at the side. Two of the braziers used in severe weather near the locomotive to prevent freezing, lay in front of the lamp post. The small turntable can be seen at the end.

Huntingdon locomotive shed, the coaling facility was by hand shovelling from the concrete topped platform direct into the locomotives tender. Sand for engine use was kept in the metal bin. No water crane existed at the depot although water was available from a hosepipe. The line on the far right crossed an inspection pit and led to the small turntable. Only a few times can I recall seeing more than one locomotive at the shed. This was on the rare occasions of a failed engine awaiting return to Cambridge depot.

The Travelling Post Office trains (TPOs) still run in various parts of the country. Although collection and despatch of mail at speed has not taken place for many years. During the fifties Huntingdon Post Office was responsible for mail service on three trains, the 'London-York-Edinburgh TPO' and 'North Eastern TPO' up and down trains. This picture shows the first installation on the down line (one of four) only the first having the net for collection of mail pouches. The twin arm set behind was to be found at all four sites, enabling eight heavy leather pouches to be despatched to the TPO. Depending on the make up of the train several pouches could be dropped at Huntingdon. Mail from Cambridge was also handled here. (1 March 1954).

Track laying on the East Coast Main Line fifties style. No. 12126 was in charge of the Engineers' train relaying the 'up main' on the 30 January 1955. The use of a diesel locomotive was rather unusual on this duty as on most occasions a J6 0-6-0 from New England or Hitchin depots was the normal motive power.

For many years a J15 class 0-6-0 was allocated to Huntingdon on a ten day rota basis from Cambridge shed. The duty was widely known as the 'Huntingdon Pilot'. Other than shunting the locomotive also worked a goods to and from St Ives. For a short period a duty working a pick up goods to St Neots was added. On more than one occasion the 'Pilot' was commandeered to take over a heavy express from a failed locomotive. Just what the main line crew thought of the J15 on a thirteen coach express when it replaced their A4 'Pacific' is not known. The gallant J15 struggled to St Neots – where a V2 replaced it. No. 65474 was in the busy yard on 6 August 1954.

Huntingdon No. 1 signal box was the larger of the two, apart from main line duties it controlled the goods yards also the Kettering - Cambridge line, this was a single track operated by a 'token'. The walkway to enable the change over of tokens to be completed can easily be seen on the left of the picture.

Huntingdon No. 2 signal box was at the north end of the station. Behind the box was a Huntingdonshire County Council Highways depot, when this picture was taken on the 18 September 1955. Engineering work had recently taken place on the 'up main' as the 70m.p.h. speed restriction warning sign indicates.